Trains and Their Rails

By Cameron Macintosh

T0360239

Contents

Kinds of Trains

Trains can take us
a long way.

We can gaze at lakes
and hills.

Lots of kids ride on
this big train.

Yay!

Hold on and be safe!

Some kids take a train
to school.

This long train is very quick.

And it is very safe.

It has good brakes!

This long train is not as quick.

But it can take lots of things
a long way.

We pack things in crates
and put them on the train.

crates

Rails

Trains run on rails.

Two rails make a track.

rails

track

A train has many wheels.

Its wheels stay on the rails.

wheels

To be safe, stay back
from the rails.

Do **not** play on train tracks!

Take a Train

We get on and off the train
at a train stop.

We wait for the train
at the stop.

Do not be late.

You will miss the train!

It's fun to go on a train
with your friends!

CHECKING FOR MEANING

1. What do trains run on? *(Literal)*

2. Which part of the train stays on the rails? *(Literal)*

3. Why are trains that carry lots of things not as quick? *(Inferential)*

EXTENDING VOCABULARY

gaze	What does it mean to *gaze*? If you gaze at something, do you have a quick look or a long look? What are other words that can be used instead of *look*? E.g. glance, stare.
brakes	What are *brakes* used for on a train? Why is it important for trains to have good brakes? Which other vehicles have brakes?
crates	What is a *crate*? What items can you put in a crate? Are all crates the same size? Why do you think things are put in a crate to be moved by a train?

MOVING BEYOND THE TEXT

1. What other ways do children travel to school apart from on a train?

2. How is it different travelling on a train than in a plane?

3. What other vehicles run on rails? What is a monorail? Have you travelled on a monorail?

4. How can you stay safe at train stops and near train tracks?

SPELLINGS FOR THE LONG /a/ VOWEL SOUND

| ay | ai | a_e | a | ea | eigh |

PRACTICE WORDS

Trains

way

train

Yay

rails

stay

play

wait

take

gaze

lakes

safe

brakes

crates

late

make

Take

Rails